The Secret Revealed

Paul Szatkowski

www.SafeHomePurchase.com

Dedication

This work is dedicated to my family; my wife LaDonna whose strength has been my inspiration and my children Brandon, Joshua, and Sarah. Thanks to my Lord and Savior, Jesus Christ for this opportunity to help make a difference in peoples lives. Through him all things are possible.

John 15:5b"....apart from me you can do nothing"

Disclaimer

This information is designed to provide accurate and authoritative information in regard to the subject matter covered. It is offered with the understanding that the author is not engaged in rendering legal, accounting, or other professional service. If legal advice or other expert advice is required, the services of a competent professional should be sought.   The information, ideas, and suggestions contained herein have been developed from personal sources, including publications and research, that are considered to and believed reliable but cannot be guaranteed insofar as they apply to a particular persons situation.

TABLE OF CONTENTS

Chapter 1
Introduction

It was a Friday night and we sorely needed a break from the weekly routine. We set out for a quick bite to eat and then off to the movie theatre. This was a rare occasion for us of late and something didn't quite feel right. There was this guilty feeling we couldn't seem to shake. It lingered like one of the many dark gray clouds of a Michigan winter. That cloud followed us from the restaurant to the movie theatre. The thought of spending $40 for a night out just didn't seem right.

The movie "Click" featuring Adam Sandler had reached the part where he was face down in the parking lot in the pouring rain yelling for his kids to come back so he could tell them that he loved them both. It dawned on me at that moment how we had not only been robbed of our money but also of the precious time that could have been spent with the ones we love. Would that somehow resemble us in years to come, regretting all of the time this incident had stolen from us?

It was at that moment I leaned over to LaDonna and whispered that I was light headed, and was about to pass out. I put my head on her shoulder and then her lap when things went completely dark. She somehow remained calm while I was out. This had never happened to me before under any circumstances. I was in excellent physical health for a 42 year old. As the movie ended we sat in the empty theatre until I was able to stand and walk out. After the movie she insisted on taking me to the emergency room, but I refused. The next morning I finally gave in and had an EKG and blood work completed. Everything checked out normal and the Doctors were left shrugging their shoulders.

My personal diagnosis was that I suffered a stress attack from the mounting pressure this situation had caused that was triggered by this climax point in the movie.

Another even more serious incident happened to LaDonna one evening when she got up from bed for a drink of water. On her way back to bed she had passed out and hit the dresser. I quickly sprang from sleep to her side where I picked her up and put her back in bed. She almost immediately passed out again.

I yelled at the top of my lungs for my son who sprang from his bed to help. I told him to call 911 and get me a cold towel. All I could do was elevate her feet to get the blood back into her head. She regained consciousness and I ordered my Son to cancel the ambulance. I monitored her for the remaining hours of the early morning until the sun came up. When we told the receiving Nurse what had happened they quickly expedited us back to see the Doctor's. A battery of test were performed including blood work, EKG, CAT scan. We breathed a sigh of relief when the "all clear" was given. There had been talk about the potential for a tumor, brain aneurism. To this day, the Doctors still don't know why this happened.

We both begun to reflect on events leading up to this. LaDonna shared her fear of our financial situation. She went on to say how she didn't know how we were going to recover from this. Our case had just been turned down by the trial judge and we now had no choice but to appeal. This meant it would cost even more money and take more precious time, all while the debt continued to mount. These two personal incidences are being shared as examples of the physical and emotional stress this situation has caused in our lives. Together we agreed that we can't let this effect us in this way. We have children who still need us. We also agreed to put our complete faith in Jesus and our belief that he is in total control.

Although it is not perfectly clear why we were chosen to go through this and what God fully expects from us, we remain committed to listen and to be obedient. We go forward on faith and continue to seek strength in our Lord. With him we know we will get through this.

Finally, we agreed to support each other and to keep working our recovery strategy while trying to maintain a positive attitude.

Thankfully our relationship has remained strong through this ordeal. We have certainly had our moments like most couples but at our core we love each other very much. We believe God has put us together as a couple and we are committed to each other. Now we are a man and women on a mission to educate home buyers and sellers of the unknown risk that exist at the closing table. In this book we share the industry secret so you won't have to experience the nightmare we have been living for almost three years.

Our Story

We may be smiling in the picture on this book cover but believe us we are not very happy because of what we are about to share. This is a story of a couple who formed a real estate investment business to generate additional money to fund their children's college education. The business is called PAL Properties LLC for (Paul and LaDonna). For several years things were going well until the closing funds for one deal were stolen by a Title Agent who quickly went out of business.

As home buyers we did the ONLY thing we thought we could do to protect ourselves. We purchased title insurance. The Title Insurance Company (Ticor Title) however will not stand behind the claim as you are about to read. As you can imagine this incident has rocked our world beyond comprehension.

Now you might be thinking: This can't happen to me? Our State will protects us, right? We close through an Attorney. I would march down there and demand my money back! What you about to learn is that this risk is very real and happens more frequently than people know.

We are about to share the industry secret of how Title Insurance Underwriters protect the money of Banks during the real estate transaction against any wrong doings by their Title Agents/ Attorneys but they <u>do not</u> provide protection for consumers, unless you know the secret.

LaDonna is a Real Estate Agent in Michigan and Georgia, and Loan Closing Specialist with a Bachelor Degree in Finance. She works for a regional bank. I am an automotive marketing professional with an MBA and passion for real estate. I work for the worlds largest automotive finance company.

Together we have been real estate investors for over 12 years and have received some of the best training in the business. We both have attended numerous seminars, real estate training courses and are members of various real estate investment clubs. In 2005 we had 22 buy/sell transactions with single family homes and duplexes. We specialized in foreclosures, buying via short sale at a discount then reselling at a discount to move the properties quickly. The sky appeared to be the limit! Then it happened.......

We bought a foreclosure in a Southeast Michigan suburb and paid $125,000 cash for the property using funds from investors. Quickly we cleaned up the home, purchased some appliances and found a Lease Option buyer for the home. We stood to make a nice profit of $30,000 on the deal once the Lease Option Buyer completed the purchase. In the mean time we would collect a modest positive cash flow on the property and work to get the buyer into a mortgage as quickly as possible.

Everything was going as planned until we attempted to finance the home about 60 days later and pull out the original investment money. The bank called and said we were not showing on title? Immediately we called the Title Agency but kept getting the answering machine.

Frustrated, we contacted the Title Insurance Company, (Ticor Title) with whom we purchased Title Insurance through when we bought the home.

Ticor informed us that their Title Agency was out of business and directed us to one of their other Title Agencies to have the Warranty

Deed signed and recorded a second time. Problem handled, so we thought until we discovered that the bank we purchased the home from (who was holding the existing lien from the seller) received a check from the Title Agent but it had came back NSF... Non-Sufficient Funds!

They never received the payoff on the existing lien therefore they did not release the mortgage on the home. Bottom line... we paid for the house but didn't own it. The bank still owned it and the Title Agent took our money and was out of business!

Once again we contacted the Title Insurance Company (Ticor) to file a claim. It was quickly denied on the basis that the Title Agent was only a Issuing/sales agent not an escrow agent and they were not responsible for their acts. So the bottom line is that the Title Agency stole our money along with others and went out business. We did the only thing we could which was to buy Title Insurance. The Title Agents insurance company Zurich would not stand behind their Errors and Omissions policy since fraud was involved. Of course the owner of the Title Agency was broke and faced federal charges.

This began a long, costly legal battle which we are still involved with today. This traumatic event has caused a tremendous amount of anxiety, financial hardship and has robbed us not only of the money but of our quality of life. The silver lining for us revolves around 1) Our faith and relationship in Jesus as Lord and Savior has been strengthened and 2) we are committed to driving change to protect others with all that we have learned. The lessons we have learned are not widely known but need to be. What happened to us should not happen to anyone and we can help prevent that.

Taking The High Road

In this book you will learn what you need to do to protect yourself and your family when buying a home. We have uncovered the loopholes and little secrets that Title Insurance Companies and Title Agents/Attorneys don't want you to know about.

If this can happen to two people who are as involved in the business as we are then it can happen to anyone. Including YOU!

Make no mistake about it. What happened to us, happens to people throughout the United States and no one is doing anything about it. Consumers (Home Buyers & Sellers) are left to fend for themselves against giant corporations to recover their hard earned money.

It is time to build awareness for this major risk and to drive change in the industry so home buyers can achieve the American Dream of home ownership without this major risk. Building awareness of this issue we believe will help us in our legal battle and hopefully we will have warned thousands of innocent people so escrow theft does not happen to them.

Please recognize that the information provided in this book will help you avoid a similar situation to ours but there is no 100% guarantee that nothing bad will ever happen. Even banks that are FDIC insured to protect money up to $100,000.00 are subject to the backing of the US government.

An Industry Secret Revealed

This is not a book about having your home inspected, properly surveyed, appraised, or a lesson in real estate contract law or lending. Those are all very important steps that should be handled carefully by reputable professionals. The purpose of this book is to raise awareness and drive change in the industry for a little known, yet major risk to consumers in the home buying process.

As the Closing Process diagram below indicates, when you buy a home or parcel of land your money is being handed to an intermediary who is conducting the closing. Typically it will either be a Title Agent or Closing Attorney. As the buyer you will bring certified funds to closing for down payment, closing cost, or maybe you are paying cash. The Title Agent/Attorney then processes the money, receiving and dispensing thousands of checks each month. They will pay lien holders, tax bills, water companies, home owner associations etc.. They do this without a lot of oversight or regulation. This can create a major problem should your funds be purposefully mishandled.

There is no one, let me repeat...NO ONE standing behind you to reimburse your money if someone mishandles the money on purpose, unless you have taken specific actions prior to closing on the property.

THE CLOSING PROCESS

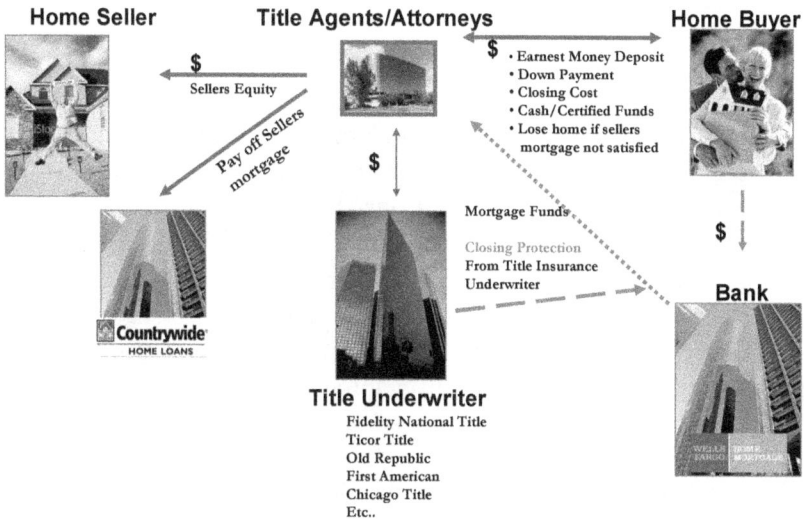

Title Insurance Companies <u>will</u> stand behind and provide closing protection of the funds from large Lenders such as Countrywide, Chase, Wells Fargo, etc if anything is done incorrectly by the Title Agency or Closing Attorney the money they have involved in the transaction will be protected. Consumers on the other hand are NOT protected against wrong doings by the Agents and Attorneys such as money theft, defalcation, or embezzlement.

Consumers pay large premiums for Title Insurance, these companies conveniently wash their hands of their Agents actions stating that they are only issuing agents. Ticor Title Insurance is a perfect example. They provide their Agents with an Escrow Accounting Standards manual, they have the right to audit their books as necessary, take control of the Agents escrow accounts, change locks, confiscate all the files and hard drives. Yet they claim they have no control and are not responsible for their Agents actions who may have mishandled your money. Does it sound like a double standard to you? **ABSOLUTELY!**

Chapter 2

The Deal

An individual at the Title Agency where we did all of our closings approached us about his personal home that was about to go into foreclosure. He said he couldn't afford to make the payments any longer, hasn't been able to sell it, and needs out. He had witnessed firsthand the help we provided to numerous people that year which gave him the confidence we could help him as well. It is a great feeling after a closing to have people that were in a very difficult situation of losing their home or to shake your hand or give you a hug and say "Thank You, you don't know how much we appreciate you helping us out".

Of course we agreed to help this young man out with his property. We had him sign the necessary paperwork and began the process. After about 45 days the banks accepted our offer. There was a first mortgage with Chase for $148,712 and a second mortgage with EMC for $35,400. Each lender accepted a much lower offer a discount totaling over $63,000.00 on the original mortgages. This represented a good discount especially given the facts that the home was a 3 bedroom brick, in good shape, which didn't need any major repairs. We simply ordered a dumpster and had the garage and yard cleaned out.

We then installed a new washer and dryer. This house was considered really clean for a foreclosure. We put a sign in the yard and had it leased with an option to purchase for $169,000.00 to a young lady who had a good job but below average credit. We put her on a credit restoration program and began working with her to clean things up and get into a loan as soon as possible. We stood to net over $30,000.00 on the deal after all closing cost and some seller concessions were paid. Overall a really good deal for the home owner , the bank, and us.

Chapter 3
The Closing

Our going in objective for each real estate deal was to have a buyer for the property at the time we purchased the home via short sale. It was not uncommon for us to purchase the home from the seller in foreclosure in one room then a few minutes later go into the conference room next door at the Title Agent and sell it to our buyer. It takes a lot of communication to get both buyer and seller to the Title Agency closing table the same time.

The lender for your home buyer may have certain requirements such as the home seller must have owned the home for 6-12 months before reselling it. In the lenders mind this helps protect them against false appraisals and limits their risk from funding a home that really isn't worth the appraised amount. We would do our best to have our home buyers finance with certain lenders who did not have these types of "seasoning of title" requirements. In some cases we have had shared our acceptance letters with the banks and explain in detail that the home was bought via short sale. Most lenders were fine once they understood how we were purchasing the home and why we would only own it for a short period.

For this particular closing we did not have the home pre-sold before the closing, but the equity spread was great enough to justify us moving forward with the deal. We opted to pay cash for this home from private investor financing and then finance the home later to pull the cash out.

Title Commitment

The title commitment is not something you should gloss over.
Review it carefully for liens, past due taxes, list of exceptions, etc. In
our case the commitment list of exceptions shows that outstanding
liens for Chase and EMC.

This is a very important point in our particular case. Ticor has
argued that in order for an actual Title Insurance policy to be issued
all of the requirements listed on the Title Commitment must be
satisfied. In fact they have stated in some of their pleadings that it is
up to us, (the consumer) to ensure all exceptions are satisfied.

Our argument as consumers is that it is their Agents responsibility to
satisfy these liens so long as we give them the money to do so. The
reality is that as a home buyer or seller we show up a the closing table
to sign the necessary documents, provide the necessary closing funds,
line up the necessary financing and purchase title insurance to protect
ourselves. After closing, we walk away with the keys to our new
home without any worry. No one has ever warned us about the risk
that exist with Title Agents/Attorneys who handle billions of dollars
annually with very little regulation.

Ticor states that if the exceptions of the Title Commitment are not
satisfied their Title Insurance Policy will not be issued. In a later
chapter we will show you some steps to help reduce your risk in this
area. For now, you must review the Title Commitment and
understand not only the exceptions listed but also the liens that exist.

Title Commitment

TICOR TITLE INSURANCE COMPANY
COMMITMENT

SCHEDULE A

OFFICE FILE #:	2005110102	REINSURANCE #:	
AGENT ID #:	MI2373	PROPOSED OWNER AMOUNT:	$120,695.00
COMMITMENT #:	2005110102	PROPOSED LOAN AMOUNT:	$
STATE:	Michigan	EFFECTIVE DATE:	August 25, 2005

1. Policy or Policies to be issued:

   ALTA LOAN POLICY   (ALTA Loan Policy (10/17/92))
   Proposed Insured:

   ALTA OWNER'S POLICY   (ALTA Own. Policy (10/17/92))
   Proposed Insured:

   Pal Properties, LLC

   Proposed Insured:

2. The estate or interest in the land described or referred to in the Commitment and covered herein is: Fee Simple and is at the effective date hereof vested in:

   Ronald M. Lucas, Jr., a single man, subject to the interest of Mortgage Electronic Registration Systems, Inc., pursuant to Sheriff's Deed dated September 7, 2005

3. The land referred to in this Commitment is described as follows:

   SEE EXHIBIT A ATTACHED HERETO

   Issued By: Consolidated Title Services, LLC
   20300 Civic Center Dr. Suite 302
   Southfield, MI 48076

   _____
   Consolidated Title Services, LLC

NOTE: This Commitment consists of insert pages labeled Schedules A, Schedule B - Section 1, and Schedule B - Section 2. This Commitment is of no force and effect unless both pages are included with any added pages incorporated by reference.

TICOR TITLE INSURANCE COMPANY
COMMITMENT

Commitment #: 2005110102

File #:   2005110102

SCHEDULE B - SECTION 2

EXCEPTIONS

Schedule B of the policy or policies to be issued will contain exceptions to the following matters unless the same are disposed of to the satisfaction of the Company.

1. Defects, liens, encumbrances, adverse claims or other matters, if any, created, first appearing in the public records or attaching subsequent to the effective date hereof but prior to the date the proposed Insured acquires for value of record the estate or interest or mortgage thereon covered by this Commitment.

2. Rights or claims of parties in possession not shown by the public records.

3. Encroachments, overlaps, boundary line disputes, and any other matters which would be disclosed by an accurate survey-and inspection of the premises.

4. Easements or claims of easements not shown by the public records.

5. Taxes or special assessments which are not shown as existing liens by the public records.

6. Taxes and assessments for the year and subsequent years, as well as the lien for any additional taxes for prior years due to reassessments or rebillings.

7. TAXES - 2005 WINTER TAX $2,672.51, DUE PAID   TAX ID: 42-006-01-0012-000   TAXES - 2005 SUMMER TAX $2,160.92, SEV$64,700.00

8. SUBJECT TO A PROPERLY EXECUTED WARRANTY DEED FROM RONALD M. LUCAS, Jr. AND SPOUSE, IF ANY TO PAL PROPERTIES, LLC.

9. MORTGAGE: EXECUTED BY RONALD M. LUCAS, JR., A SINGLE MAN TO HOLDER FIELDSTONE MORTGAGE COMPANY IN THE AMOUNT OF $141,600.00, DATED 11/24/2003, RECORDED 12/03/2003, LIBER 39689, PAGE 1187, WAYNE COUNTY RECORDS. OPEN ENDED: NO

10. MORTGAGE: EXECUTED BY RONALD M. LUCAS, JR., A SINGLE MAN TO HOLDER FIELDSTONE MORTGAGE COMPANY IN THE AMOUNT OF $35,400.00, DATED 11/24/2003, RECORDED 12/03/2003, LIBER 39689, PAGE 1208, WAYNE COUNTY RECORDS. OPEN ENDED: NO

11. FAILURE TO MEET REQUIREMENTS WILL RESULT IN NON-ISSUANCE OF TITLE INSURANCE POLICY.

12. ANY EASEMENT, AS SHOWN ON RECORDED PLAT OR OF RECORD.

13. BUILDING AND USE RESTRICTIONS, AGREEMENTS AND EASEMENTS OF PUBLIC RECORD.

14. COVENANTS, CONDITIONS AND RESTRICTIONS, IF ANY, EASEMENTS OR SERVITUDES, ANY LEASE GRANT, EXCEPTION OR RESERVATION OF MINERAL RIGHTS APPEARING IN THE PUBLIC RECORD.

15. SCHEDULE B, SECTION 2, ITEM ONE IS HEREBY DELETED UPON THE UNDERSTANDING THAT THE COMPANY'S TITLE POLICY ISSUING AGENT, CONSOLIDATED TITLE SERVICES, L.L.C., WILL CONDUCT THE SETTLEMENT AND DISBURSE FUNDS IN THIS TRANSACTION AND IS SUBJECT TO THE FOLLOWING: 1.   A SEARCH COMMENCING WITH THE EFFECTIVE DATE OF THIS COMMITMENT THROUGH THE LATEST AVAILABLE TITLE EVIDENCE WILL BE PERFORMED IMMEDIATELY PRIOR TO SETTLEMENT. IF THIS SEARCH REVEALS A TITLE DEFECT OF OTHER OBJECTIONABLE MATTERS, AN ENDORSEMENT WILL BE ISSUED REQUIRING THAT SUCH DEFECT OR OBJECTION BE CLEARED PRIOR TO SETTLEMENT.   2.   UPON SETTLEMENT, THE CLOSING

Chapter 4
Things Start To Unravel

When we began the financing to pull out the original cash investment the bank we were financing with contacted us to say there was a problem. First, we were not showing up on Title and second, there were taxes owed on the home which should have been paid at closing by the Title Agent.

We tried calling the Title Agent numerous times but kept getting their answering service. The Title Agent, Consolidated Title Services (CTS) had gone out of business so we contacted Ticor Title Insurance to file a claim. Initially there was not a lot of panic. We assumed there was a mix up that could be corrected.

Since CTS was out of business Ticor directed us to another one of their Title Agents (Andover Title) to have the warranty deed refiled. The seller of the home met us at Andover Title to sign the warranty deed again and have it notarized. At that time we requested a letter from the Title Agent stating that they had in fact recorded the Deed along with a receipt showing the transfer tax and recording fees had been paid. The letter was to be used to secure the financing we needed since it could take months for the deed to reflect in public records.

Our initial claim was filed for reimbursement of the taxes and fees we had to pay as a result of re-filing the Warranty Deed. Ticor quickly responded with a rejection letter. In shock and disbelief we quickly interviewed a number of Attorneys and selected one who was knowledgeable on the subject, honest, and reasonably priced. Fortunately for us we later discovered our Attorney was a strong Christian who actually attended our church. Probably why we were drawn to the legal services of Rod Dunlap in the first place.

A Bigger Problem Realized

When we discovered that Chase had not released the mortgage we immediately called them to find out why. This was one of the worst calls we have ever taken. Chase told us that the check for the mortgage payoff had bounced. NSF- Non Sufficient Funds ! How could this be right? The Title Agents check had bounced and Chase was not about to discharge the mortgage.

Chase never contacted us to alert us of the problem and neither did Ticor. Ticor Title Insurance Underwriters had known after their audit in December 2005 that this check was going to bounce. They spent days reconciling Consolidated Title Services books yet didn't bother to notify us. They knew exactly what had happened and the predicament we were in and the fact that the check had not cleared. Yet they purposefully concealed this information from us.

Wouldn't you think there would be an obligation on their part to warn those impacted by their Agents wrong doings. If not a legal obligation then certainly a moral obligation exist. A simple letter, phone call, email or fax from Ticor would have allowed us to limit our damages. We were busily fixing up and marketing the home to find a lease option buyer for the home. We could have minimized and maybe recovered completely from the damage had they informed us of their findings.

If you look closely at the check it appears Chase apparently attempted to cash the Consolidated Title check twice. Had they tried a third time it may have gone through since we later learned that an escrow balance of $171,000.00 existed at the time Ticor allegedly took control of the accounts.

NSF Check

Account:8000041270 Serial:77283 Amount:$119,695.00 Sequence:1031760290 TR:72406768 TranCode:100 Date:12-15-2005

Once again we contacted Ticor to file an amended claim. They quickly denied this claim stating many of the same reasons in their denial of the tax reimbursement claim where we discovered the Deed had not been recorded.

They also stated we did not have a Closing Protection Letter (CPL), that Consolidated Title Services (CTS) was only an issuing agent and they were not responsible for the actions of CTS.

Finally Ticor said that we (the home buyer) were responsible for ensuring that the liens listed on the Title Commitment were paid off. How can that be? We handed their Title Agent the money to pay all existing liens and it was their Agents responsibility to do that.

Ticor claims to be the largest Title Insurance Underwriter in the country. They belong to Fidelity Financial Services headquartered out of Jacksonville Florida. They state on their website that they pride themselves in focusing on the customer and their $940 million in reserves. Now that should make you feel comfortable that they are going to be there for you, right. Wrong. Obviously in our case their words speak louder than their actions.

So what is driving them to fight so hard in this case? We suspect that if they lose this case it could expose them to broader liability for the acts of their Agent network. They apparently have millions of dollars at stake. So why not just pay our claim to keep this from being decisioned against them in the courts? Little do they know that we are committed to driving change within the industry if they don't fix this.

Ticor's Second Rejection

🏛 TICOR TITLE INSURANCE

Writer's Direct Dial: (312) 223-2894
Writer's Direct Fax: (312) 223-2559
Email: rgellersted@FNF.com

February 13, 2006

Rod Dunlap, Esq.
37000 Grand Ave., Suite 230
Farmington Hills, MI 48335

RE: Ticor Claim No.:   205825
       Proposed Insured: Pal Properties, LLC
       Property: 20049 Huntington Ave:, Harper Woods, Wayne County,
                               MI 48225
       Commitment No.:   2005110102

Dear Mr. Dunlap:

Ticor Title Insurance Company ("Ticor") has reviewed your amended claim made and has come to a coverage determination. For the reasons stated below, your claim is respectfully denied.

You seek reimbursement from Ticor as a result of Escrow actions on the part of the closing agent, Consolidated Title Services, LLC, ("CTS") who closed your purchase on November 28, 2005. Specifically, it is the failure to make payment out of your funds as purchaser for the following as indicated on the RESPA:

Payoff of First Mortgage To Chase Home Finance, LLC, $ 119,695.00.

According to the RESPA, you purchased for cash and no purchase money mortgage financed the purchase. CTS was an agent of Ticor only for the issuance of title insurance and not for any other purposes. CTS is not an escrow agent of Ticor. My records indicate that no Closing Protection Letter was furnished to you as purchaser nor was one requested. Closing Protection Letters, when issued provide for indemnification as a result of the escrow negligence of an agent. As a result of No Closing Protection Letter having been issued, Ticor's sole basis of liability to you, if any, is under the Ticor Commitment.

The Ticor Commitment contained effective date August 25, 2005. Schedule B-Section I contained the following requirements:

10.   Record Discharge of Mortgage Recorded In Liber 39689, Page
       1187, Wayne County Records.

Schedule B – Section 2 stated the following:

Schedule B of the policy or policies to be issued will contain exceptions to the following matters unless the same are disposed of to the satisfaction of the Company.

9.   Mortgage executed by Ronald M. Lucas, Jr., a single man to holder Fieldstone Mortgage Company in the amount of $ 141,600.00, dated 11/24/2003, recorded 12/03/2003 Liber 39689, Page 1187, Wayne County Records: Open Ended: No.

11.   Failure to Meet Requirements will result in non-issuance of title insurance policy.

The mortgage recorded at Liber 39689, Page 1187 contained a power of sale and a Sheriff's Deed was made September 7, 2005 and recorded at Liber 43333, Page 346, Wayne County Records. The redemption period runs to March 7, 2006. During our telephone conversation, I recall you saying that Chase Home Finance foreclosed and this was my understanding. The mortgage to be paid off that foreclosed was the same mortgage excepted under the commitment.

Based on the facts and commitment provisions referred to, we must respectfully deny your client's claim. If you are aware of facts or an interpretation of the policy which would alter this conclusion, please provide that information to me in writing within 30 days of the date of this letter. Although the reasons stated above are sufficient to deny the claim, they are not intended to be exclusive. Ticor Title Insurance Company reserves the right to establish additional grounds for denial should a further review of the file become necessary. If I receive no written response from you, I will close your file in 30 days.

Sincerely,

Richard Gellersted
Vice President & Senior Claims Counsel

RG.rg

2

22

Escrow Account Balance

A review of the bank records for Consolidated Title show that there was in fact $171,000.00 remaining in the escrow account at the time Ticor shut their Agent down.

With the Title Agent now out of business what else is the nations largest Title Underwriter to do? Allegedly take control of the remaining money in the escrow account. The depositions from Consolidated Titles owner and employees indicate that control of the escrow account was turned over to a Ticor representative at the conclusion of the audit. We know of one other consumer and we suspect some large lenders also lost funds. Were the large lenders made whole for any losses they suffered? We suspect they were quickly paid but the consumers (us and one other) were not paid for their Agents wrong doings. We did what everybody does when buying or selling a home, we purchased Title Insurance. This could have happened to anyone but instead it happened to us.

So why wouldn't Ticor just pay our claim to take care of the consumer they hold in such high regard and then subrogate against Consolidated Title and it's owner in the courts. That is a question only they can answer.

Consolidated Titles Final Escrow Account Statement

```
                                    Date  12/30/05      Page      7
                                    Primary Account   8000041270
                                    CIF Number           C003589
                                    Enclosures               241
```

PREMIUM BUSINESS CHECKING   8000041270   (Continued)

Daily Balance Information

Date	Balance	Date	Balance	Date	Balance
12/14	171,011.00	12/15	171,011.00	12/16	.00

* * * END OF STATEMENT * * *

Balance in Consolidated Titles escrow account at the time Ticor shut their Agent down

Chapter 5
Lawsuit Filed

In the planning stages of this book we considered including copies of all legal filings, briefs, case evaluations and the courts rulings. Including these would create a book three to four inches thick making it too costly to communicate what you really need to know. We can make all of the legal filings available to you just by contacting us directly. In the end, we felt we could communicate the key messages without their inclusion.

In short, Ticor attempts to completely wash their hands of any responsibility. They state that they are not responsible for any of Consolidated Title Services (CTS) actions since they were only and issuing agent and not a Direct Operations (escrow agent) for them.

Ticor also claims we were not issued a Closing Protection Letter (CPL). The CPL protects lenders and consumers from the mishandling of funds by the title agents by having the Title Insurance Underwriter, such as Ticor stand behind any claims. This can be provided when Title Insurance is purchased. This is a FREE piece of paper just for the asking. Yet most consumers don't know anything about it. <u>This is the little secret Title Underwriters don't really care for you to know</u>. When a Lenders Title Policy is purchased at closing, the Lenders providing a mortgage require Title Underwriters to also provide closing protection on all of their funds involved in the transaction. Even though consumers pay large premiums for Title Insurance, these companies will not stand behind any mishandling of funds by their Agents or Closing Attorneys.

Ticor provides their Agents with an Escrow Accounting Standards Manual, they have the right to audit their books as necessary, take control of the Agents escrow bank accounts, change locks on the doors of their Agents offices, and confiscate all the files and hard drives in order to protect themselves. Yet they are currently afforded the luxury of **not** being held accountable for their agents actions.

You have heard the old saying " Having your cake and eating it to".
That fits perfectly with Title Insurance Underwriters and the network
of Agents they have set up to sell their insurance and perform closings.

Case Overview

To help bring clarity as to why Ticor is not claiming responsibility we
have listed their "key" defense points and then our response points.

1. TICOR DEFENSE CLAIM

Ticor claims that a "Title Commitment is not a Title Insurance Policy"

PAL PROPERTIES RESPONSE

- The State of Michigan views a Title Commitment as a "Binder" for
  Title Insurance (see attached letter from the State of MI page 30)

- PAL Properties LLC paid the premium ($708) in full to their agent
  Consolidated Title Services (CTS) at the time of closing

- Ticor was the Principal and CTS was an Agent of Ticor, therefore
  Ticor is responsible for overseeing and monitoring escrow accounts
  which they failed to do

- Ticor knew that the check CTS issued on behalf of PAL had
  bounced yet they concealed this fact. Had PAL been notified they
  could have taken action to minimize damages

- PAL did the only thing (like most consumers) they could do to
  protect themselves, they purchased Title Insurance however Ticor
  refused to issue the policy since their Agent did not pay off the
  existing liens

2. TICOR DEFENSE CLAIM

Ticor claims that they are not responsible for their Agents actions since a Closing Protection Letter (CPL) was not issued to PAL Properties at the time of closing

PAL PROPERTIES RESPONSE

- Ethan Powsner, Ticors Regional Manager testified that Ticor does not have a policy for issuing CPL' s to cash buyers

- Betsey Whitney, Office Manager from Consolidated Title also testified that Ticor does not issue CPL's for cash buyers

- Testimony from CTS employees and other Ticor Agents indicate they didn't even know a CPL could be issued to consumers

- The majority of consumers buying a home do not even know what a Closing Protection Letter is or why they should ask for one

3. TICOR DEFENSE CLAIM

Consolidated Title was only an Issuing Agent and not a Direct Operations (Escrow Agent) for Ticor

PAL PROPERTIES RESPONSE

- There are several past legal cases that show the inherent responsibility that Principles (such as Ticor) have for their Agents

- If Consolidated was ONLY an issuing agent, how is it that Ticor could allegedly take control of Consolidated escrow accounts, files and change the locks on their office doors

- Ticor did not properly monitor Consolidated or properly respond to notification of an escrow imbalance prior to our closing. Ticor was alerted to an escrow shortage in May 2005 but failed to take corrective action

- Ticor made Consolidated follow all of their escrow procedures and processes outlined in their Escrow Standards Manual as required in the Agency agreement

- Ticor's Regional Manager Ethan Powsner testified that notifying the customers who were going to have checks bounce **"would be a nice service to offer"** but they don't do this

- Ticor allegedly took control of CTS Escrow account balance of $171,000. There were a total of four bank accounts in which the whereabouts are under investigation by the Michigan Office of Financial and Insurance Regulation

- Ticor paid out over $750,000 in other claims from Lenders and mortgage companies but not to consumers related to this case

- Ticor had authority to audit the books of CTS whenever they deemed necessary however they <u>did not</u> do so after being notified in May 2005 of an escrow shortage

- Ticor Maintained more day to day control than they lead one to believe per the depositions from CTS Management

State Insurance Regulatory Agency

In the event you experience problems with your purchase or sale we strongly suggest you immediately contact your state insurance regulatory agency. State Agency names will differ depending on where you live. In some states it may be the Department of Insurance (DOI), or Office of Financial and Insurance Regulation (OFIR), Department of Financial and Professional Regulation. Keep in mind that they are dealing with dozens of issues at any given time and the regulation regarding this issue is limited to available resources.

This Michigan Office of Financial and Insurance Regulation OFIR has been and ally throughout this. The down side is they move very slow since they deal with numerous State issues. We set up a face to face meeting with an investigator and his supervisor to discuss our situation and lay out a plan. When we discovered how prevalent escrow theft is there was actually some harsh feelings toward the state for allowing this to occur, not being proactive like some other states such as Ohio.

In our case, Michigan OFIR provided a letter that says they view a title commitment as a binder on the Title Insurance Policy. This countered one of the Ticor defense points, but fell on deaf ear with the trial court judge. OFIR has been aware of the problem of escrow theft for years but has not done anything about it. They actually have been waiting for a case (like ours) to garner support internally to drive change. This is all well and good but we wish they had fixed the problem years ago so we didn't have to go through this. That said, they are trying to help by submitting an Amicus Brief on our behalf as well as subpeoning the Title Agents bank records from Ticor for investigation. We have also met with them to lay the ground work for drafting legislation to protect consumers. Our goal is to have Michigan become the model for the rest of the country.

State of Michigan's Position on Title Commitment As A Binder

JENNIFER M. GRANHOLM
GOVERNOR

STATE OF MICHIGAN
OFFICE OF FINANCIAL AND INSURANCE SERVICES
DEPARTMENT OF LABOR & ECONOMIC GROWTH
ROBERT W. SWANSON, DIRECTOR

LINDA A. WATTERS
COMMISSIONER

June 29, 2006

Mr. Paul Szatkowski
23153 Mystic Forest
Novi, MI 48375

RE: Title Commitment

Dear Mr. Szatkowski:

Thank you for your communication of June 28, 2006. You have asked for the position of the Office of Financial and Insurance Services (OFIS) on the issuance of a title commitment and whether it is looked upon as a binder for title insurance.

Section 7304 (MCL 500.7304) allows title insurers to issue "commitments for the title insurance policies specifying the requirements for the issuance of such policies." Due to the fact that some title insurance policies are not issued for up to six months or a year after the closing of a settlement service, OFIS has relied upon the representations in the commitment as a true reflection of the actual title policy. Essentially, the commitment is a unilateral contract which binds the title insurance underwriter to certain obligations.

Should you have any additional questions, please contact me.

Sincerely,

Randy A. Watkins, Certified Investigator
Senior Regulation Specialist
Insurance & Examinations Section

Street/Overnight Delivery Address: 611 W. OTTAWA STREET, 3rd FLOOR, LANSING, MICHIGAN 48933
Mailing Address: P.O. BOX 30220, LANSING, MICHIGAN 48909-7720
www.michigan.gov • TOLL FREE (877) 999-6442 LOCAL (517) 373-0220

Attorney General Amicus Brief

Part of our recovery strategy involves the solicitation of support from recognized industry experts and associations. It has taken a tremendous amount of work, and energy to reach the decision makers within the State of Michigan. Fortunately they recognized the issue at hand within the state and were willing to support us by submitting what's called an Amicus Brief. We believe this adds significantly credibility and attention to our case. We are now working with them to place a request for the support via an Amicus Brief with the National Association of Insurance Commissioners (NAIC).

Within their Amicus Brief the State provides numerous past case citations which support the obligation that exist between Principle-Agent. This relationship shows that Principles (like Ticor) are responsible for the acts of their Agents (like Consolidated Title Services). Within the filings there is much argument about which cases are applicable and which are not.

National Association of Insurance Commissioners (NAIC)

In an effort to ratchet this issue to a national level we contacted the National Association of Insurance Commissioner (NAIC). They would not budge without a request from the Michigan Insurance Commissioner. After weeks of us prodding, the state finally submitted the request to the NAIC to file an Amicus Brief on our behalf. We are awaiting their committee decision to support our case.

Ideally the NAIC will submit an Amicus Brief outlining their concerns and position on Ticor paying our claim. We are also in contact with the in-house legal counsel for the NAIC.

Michigan Association of Realtors

One of the organizations that has a vested interest in protecting consumers is the Michigan Association of Realtors (MAR). After reviewing the facts of our case they agreed to provide a letter of support. It states that they would expect Ticor to step up and protect the consumer in this case. They should be an ally in helping to communicate this issue to all Realtors in the state of Michigan. They can also assist with making this topic visible with the National Association of Realtors.

National Association of Mortgage Lenders

We have had several conference calls with this organization who is empathetic to our situation. They wanted to provide an Amicus Brief on our behalf but have resource constraints given the recent foreclosure crisis and their involvement with legislative changes. They should also provide a platform for which to communicate our situation and this topic on a national level.

Americans For Fairness In Lending

There are a number of consumer groups and one that appears to really want to offer assistance is the Americans For Fairness In Lending (AFFIL). They will help to spotlight this problem nationally by allowing us to create an "Ally" account on their website, www.affil.org to obtain greater visibility with all of their partner organizations.

Chapter 6
Issuing vs Direct Operation Agents

Let's examine the double standard that exist with Title Underwriters. A key defense point for Ticor was that the closing Title Agent was <u>only</u> an Issuing Agent and not an Escrow (Direct) Agent for Ticor. What they mean by this is that in some states Title Underwriters have direct or in-house escrow agents which are actual employees of their company. This is the safest place to have a closing done since all closing actions and money exchanged are guaranteed.

In our case the depositions revealed that Ticor was notified whenever there was an escrow imbalance. They were notified in April of 2005 of escrow imbalance problems yet failed to order an audit. It wasn't until December when it was too late did they bring in a defalcation audit team to determine the severity of the escrow imbalance that existed.

Title Agent Contract

We obtained a copy of the Agency contract between Ticor and Consolidated Title Services (CTS) the Title Agent. In this contract it does state that the Agent will use the Ticor Escrow Accounting Standards procedures. CTS was provided a copy of the Ticor Escrow Accounting Standards manual and was required to use it as part of its agency contract obligations. We were restricted from including this contract in the book but it clearly shows the depth of relationship and control that Ticor <u>has</u> over their Issuing Agents.

Within the industry the Title Underwriters have a massive distribution network to sell their title insurance. They call these Agents Issuing Agents. Ticor has the ability to audit at will, take control of escrow funds and close an agent down if they detect wrongdoings. To top it off they label them "Issuing Agents" but conveniently require that they use the Ticor Escrow Accounting Standards Manual within the contract.

The other very noticeable factor here was the lack of training provided by Ticor to their Agents. There is no mention of required training hours to ensure proper accounting or handling of paperwork. Given the volume of money handled and the existing risk you would think Ticor would require a number of training hours annually to ensure proper procedures are being followed.

Chapter 7
Trial Judge Ruling

The rulings were all made in favor of Ticor. Bottom line…we lost on every count. As you can imagine we were all stunned by this decision. Essentially the judge found Ticor not responsible for their Agents actions. It is our personal opinion that the judges decision lacked the analysis you would expect with a case of this complexity. Receiving this information was shocking and emotionally draining. We quickly reviewed our options and were advised by our Attorney that the errors made in the ruling justified that we appeal the decision.

Court of Appeals Filing

In addition to addressing the errors in the ruling which we believe were made by the judge, an additional claim of "Willful Concealment" was alleged against Ticor. They conducted an in-depth audit of Consolidated Title Services bank accounts. We are alleging they knew that the check sent to Chase to pay off the existing sellers mortgage would bounce yet did not bother to tell us. Had we known we may have been able to limit our damages. Since we filed the appeal in September 2007 it could take up to one year for the case to be reviewed.

Chapter 8

Dimensioning Escrow Theft

Escrow theft is a national issue. Several states have already taken legislative action to protect consumers. The state of Ohio recently put Senate Bill 185 into law in January 2007 which mandates that Closing Protection coverage be offered to all buyers, sellers and lenders for a nominal fee.

The chart below was provided by the Michigan Office of Financial and Insurance Regulation (OFIR). We were informed that these numbers should be considered conservative since this only provides "reported" defalcations. It clearly shows that Title Agent defalcations (fancy term for embezzlement or money theft) of escrow funds has increased significantly. It also illustrates that Title Underwriters are not standing behind their Agents defalcations. The most alarming statistic is that the dollar amount of denied claims has soared from $100,000 in 2004 to $2.4 million in 2006.

This means that in 2006 Michigan <u>consumers lost</u> a total of $2.4 million when attempting to purchase or sell a home. Finally, escrow audit frequency has decreased while the number of Title Agents has increased. Bottom line - escrow theft has grown rapidly in the last 3 years while efforts to control the problem have decreased. Michigan residents have been left having to pay the price.

	<u>2004</u>	2005	2006
Michigan Agency Defalcations	$1.4 Mil	$7.2 Mil	$7.8 Mil
Underwriter Payments due to Defalcations	$1.3	$6.8	$5.4
Defalcations not paid by Underwriters	$100,000	$400,000	$2.4 Mil
Title Agencies Owned by Underwriters	732	717	755
Agency audits by Underwriters	381	320	379
Audits as a % of total agents	52%	44%	50%

The Root Cause

Closing Agent/Attorney Payment Process

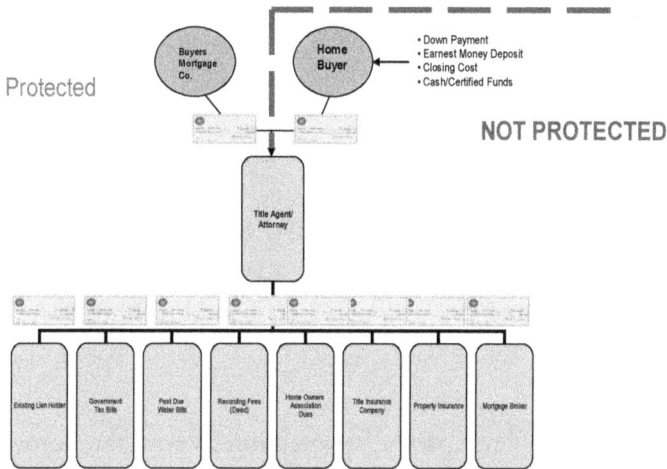

Protected

- Down Payment
- Earnest Money Deposit
- Closing Cost
- Cash/Certified Funds

Buyers Mortgage Co.

Home Buyer

NOT PROTECTED

Title Agent/ Attorney

Existing Lien Holder | Government Tax Bills | Past Due Water Bills | Recording Fees (Deed) | Home Owners Association Dues | Title Insurance Company | Property Insurance | Mortgage Broker

This illustrates how the home buyer and sellers money is not protected at closing, yet the banks and lenders are protected. This also shows the tremendous number of checks Title Agents process just for one closing. Title Agents and Closing Attorneys will average of 10-12 checks for every real estate closing transaction. Consider that a small Title Agent will average 30 closings per month, a medium Agency 70 closings monthly and a large Agency approximately 150 closings per month.

The volume of checks processed and huge flow through of dollars to the escrow accounts and then to recipients of the closing proceeds creates a great deal of room serious error. There is no way a state regulatory agency can look at every real estate transaction.

That means consumers are exposed to a significant risk with the personal money they have involved in the transaction should it be purposefully mishandled. They are also at risk of not selling or purchasing the home they thought they sold or bought if the Title Agent decides not to pay off the existing liens. This chart dimensions the volume of checks and dollar flow through for various size Title Agents.

Title Agencies	Small	Medium	Large
Average # Closings Per Mth	30	70	150
Checks Processed Mth (avg 12 per transaction)	360	840	1800
Monthly Escrow Dollar Flow Thru	$6 Mil	$14 Mil	$30 Mil
Annual Escrow Dollar Flow Thru	$72 Mil	$168 Mil	$360 Mil

Title Underwriters will not provide protection to you (the home buyer) unless you know the industry secret and take specific actions prior to purchasing the real estate.

Once you know this industry hush, hush secret, you can buy real estate with peace of mind. Understanding the specific actions to take won't cost you a dime and it may save you hundreds of thousands of dollars, and years of anxiety that can keep you from any real quality of life.

Chapter 9

Don't Let This Happen To You

We have worked with our Attorneys and industry experts to develop this chapter. There are a number of actions you must take when buying a home in order to reduce your risk. If you follow the steps we outline, you will significantly improve your odds of avoiding escrow theft. Follow them and you will receive the same protection as banks receive on their money involved with the real estate transaction.

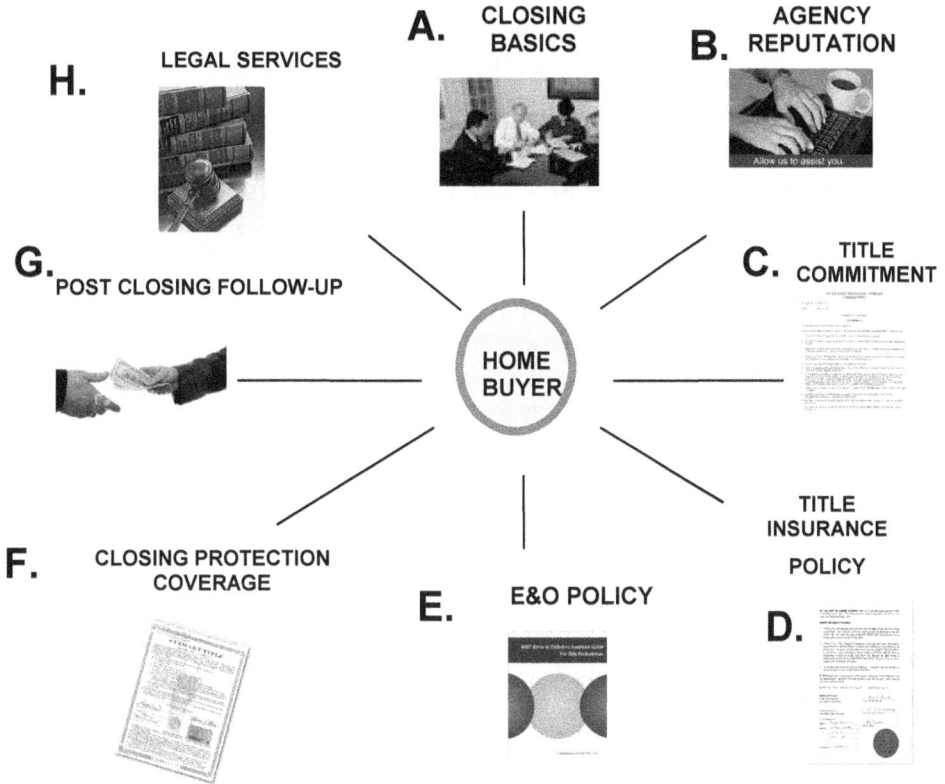

A. CLOSING BASICS

B. AGENCY REPUTATION

H. LEGAL SERVICES

G. POST CLOSING FOLLOW-UP

C. TITLE COMMITMENT

HOME BUYER

F. CLOSING PROTECTION COVERAGE

E. E&O POLICY

D. TITLE INSURANCE POLICY

A. Closing Basics

Be aware that at times Title Agents/Attorneys offices can be very fast paced environments. They make their money from closing fees and the sale of Title Insurance. So the more buyers, sellers and people refinancing flowing through their office the more money they make. Accuracy is critical and this normally means last minute changes to important documents, including the HUD 1 closing statement.

The idea here is to obtain and review the necessary closing docs in advance to avoid last minute changes. Don't be rushed at the closing table, be thorough and take whatever time you need.

Both buyers and sellers should expect to sign a lot of papers at the closing. <u>Buyers</u> might be asked to sign the following:

- A promissory note promising to pay in full the loan and interest.

- The mortgage document which secures the promissory note by giving the lender an interest in the property and the right to take and sell the property—that is, foreclose—if the mortgage payments aren't made.

- A truth in lending form which requires the lender to tell you in advance the approximate annual percentage rate of the loan over the loan's term.

- A typed loan application form.

- A payment letter telling the buyer the amount of the first payment and when it is due.

- An affidavit that the buyer's various names (if he or she has used more than one) all refer to the same person.

- A survey form stating that the buyer has seen and understands the survey of the property and that it fairly depicts the property.

- A private mortgage insurance application, usually required on loans with a down payment of less than 20 percent.

- A termite inspection or other inspection form, indicating that the buyer has seen a report of any inspections that were made.

The <u>seller</u> can expect to sign the following documents:

- The deed transferring title in the real estate from the seller to the buyer.

- A bill of sale transferring ownership of any personal property that may be included in the sale of the real estate.

- An affidavit of title in which the seller states that he or she has the legal right to sell the real estate and that there are no liens or encumbrances (judgments, mortgages, or taxes owed) on the property.

- An affidavit as to mechanic's liens and possession indicating that the seller has not had any work done on the property that would give rise to a mechanic's lien and that there are no parties other than the seller entitled to possess the property.

- An occupancy certificate indicating that a new home complies with the local housing code.

Both <u>buyer and seller</u> will also sign the following:

- An affidavit specifying the purchase price and indicating the source of the purchase price. (This affidavit assures the lender that the buyer has not received any undisclosed loans from the seller that could negatively affect the buyer's ability to repay the lender's loan.)

- A RESPA form developed by the federal Department of Housing and Urban Development and sometimes a separate closing statement, specifying all costs associated with the transaction.

What happens at the closing?

The real estate closing is the final stage in the process of buying a home. The closing is a meeting at which the buyer and seller, usually accompanied by their respective lawyers and real estate agents, complete the sale. At this meeting, the buyer usually makes all the required payments. The seller produces all documents necessary for the transfer of good—that is, marketable—title and delivers a deed that transfers the title to the buyer.

What is the closing statement?

Before the closing, the parties and their lawyers will review all documents to see that everyone is fulfilling all conditions and promises of the contract. A closing statement or settlement sheet is prepared, fully listing the financial aspects of the closing. The Real Estate Settlement Procedures Act (RESPA) will apply in any transaction in which a buyer is obtaining a federally insured mortgage from a financial institution. This requires use of a settlement sheet developed by the Department of Housing and Urban Development. In other closings in which the buyer is not obtaining a mortgage, another form of settlement sheet is usually prepared.

What are some typical closing costs? Closing costs usually include all or most of the following:

Appraisal fee

This is the fee paid for an appraisal of the property. It is required by the lender and often is paid for by the buyer. The Federal Housing Administration and Veterans Administration establish the appraisal fees for mortgages that they guarantee.

Attorney's fee

The buyer and seller pay the fee for their own lawyers. In some states, buyers are required to pay for the lender's attorney. This fee may be a certain percentage of the mortgage or a fixed fee.

Survey fee

If the lender requires a registered survey, the buyer probably will pay the fee. You may be able to avoid this fee if the lender agrees to accept a recent survey done for the seller. However, the seller must sign a document stating that the property lines have not changed since the completion of the survey and there have been no additional improvements to the property since the survey was taken. Even then, a title insurance company may require a new survey unless the survey is current or has been recertified recently.

Loan discount fee

This is the lender's charge to the buyer to obtain the loan. The buyer may have paid some of this fee in advance to secure the loan.

Inspection fees

Charges for general inspections or inspections required by local laws. The buyer or seller may be responsible for these fees depending on the contract and local law and custom.

Recording fees

The cost for recording change of ownership such as a deed; the cost of recording the buyer's mortgage; recording the release of the seller's mortgage by the seller's lender; and recording the release of any liens found in the record of title.

Title fees

Cost of title search.

Title insurance

The cost of title insurance, usually divided between the seller and buyer. The seller pays for the buyer's policy and the buyer pays for the lender's policy.

Other common fees include:

- loan origination fee to cover the lender's administrative costs in processing the loan;

- credit report fee;

- lender's appraisal fee;

- mortgage insurance application fee;

- mortgage insurance premium; and

- hazard insurance premium.

Buyers also may have to put money into escrow to assure future payment of such recurring items as real estate taxes. Also, there often are separate document fees that cover the preparation of final legal papers such as the promissory note and mortgage or deed of trust. What are some financial aspects of the closing?

At the time of closing, the seller and buyer will total up various credits in order to determine how much money the buyer must pay. The seller will receive credits for such items as unused insurance premiums, prepaid interest, and escrow deposits for insurance, taxes, and public utility charges such as water and sewer fees. These credits also will include any other items prepaid by the seller that will benefit the buyer.

The buyer normally will receive credits for such items as the earnest money deposited and taxes or special assessments that the seller has not paid. The settlement sheet also will specify who is responsible for the payment of various expenses. These will include the sales commissions and the costs of the title search, inspections, recording fees, transaction taxes, and the like.

The allocation of such expenses will depend on the terms of your contract as well as the law and customs in your area. Your real estate agent or attorney should advise you ahead of time of how much money you will need at the closing. Typically, you will be required to have a certified check in the amount required to meet these expenses.

For more closing info we suggest you visit www.homeclosing101.org to help prepare in advance of your closing.

Closing Basics - MUST HAVES

Understand the documents you will be signing and the fees being charged

---

B. Title Agency Reputation

Allow us to assist you.

So how do you know the Title Agent or Closing Attorney your Mortgage Broker or Realtor referred you to is reputable?   You can start by asking questions of the person who selected them on your behalf.

> - How long have they been in business?
>
> - Do you know the owners?
>
> - Have you heard of any complaints from any of your clients who have used them?
>
> - Are they Licensed?
>
> - How do their fees compare to other agencies?

Web Check

We suggest you visit our website at: www.SafeHomePurchase.com for the link to the Better Business Bureau to see if any complaints have been filed against the Agent.   You will also find other helpful links to help you make an educated decision.

Title Underwriter Direct Operations vs Issuing Agents

In some states Title Insurance Underwriters have "Direct Operation" Title Agents. Think of these as company owned stores staffed with their own employees. The Underwriter makes more Title Insurance premium yet they also have higher fixed expense. Since this is a Direct Operation the Underwriters will typically guarantee all aspects of your transaction. Ask in advance if your Title Agent is a Direct Operation of the Title Underwriter or just an Issuing Agent. Your money and closing transactions will have the actual Title Insurance Underwriter standing behind them. Use a Direct Operations Agent whenever possible.

Closing Instruction Checklist

This is a Closing Instruction Checklist that will help maximize your protection when closing. It will also help ferret out the bad Agents from the good as well as help your closing go smoothly. You should give this to your Title Agent/Attorney as soon as you find out with which Agent your closing will take place. We suggest you personally drop this off at the Agency in advance so you can establish a contact and get a feel for the Agency. If that is not possible fax it over to the Title Agent. **However you do it, get it in their hands and make it clear these items must be handled or there will not be a closing.**

If the Agency refuses to provide you with any of the requested information find another one. The well run professional Title Agents should comply with your request. You are their customer.

CLOSING INSTRUCTIONS

Dear Closing Department:

We will be <u>purchasing/selling</u> the home located at:

_____, and will

need the following items prior to closing.

_____1. Closing Protection Letter (CPL) from the Title Insurance
                  Underwriter made out in our name prior to closing

_____ 2. Copy of your Errors & Omissions Declaration page showing
                  date of policy expiration

_____ 3. Copy of the HUD 1 form for our review 5 days prior to closing

_____4. Copy of the Title Commitment for our review 5 days prior to
                  closing

_____5. A marked up title commitment will be required at closing showing
                  that <u>all</u> exceptions have been satisfied

_____6. Name of the Title Underwriter providing Title Insurance

_____7. Copy of the Title Insurance Policy at the time of closing

_____8. Confirmation that the funds to payoff the existing mortgage(s) have
                  been received and mortgage discharged

Please contact us at _____ when the requested
information is available so a delay in closing can be avoided.

Sincerely,

Agency Reputation - MUST HAVES

Utilize the Closing Check Sheet to maximize your protection

Use a Direct Operations Agent whenever possible instead of an Issuing Agent

C. Title Commitment

The Title Commitment may be one of the most misunderstood documents in the real estate transaction. Essentially the Title Commitment is a promise to issue an insurance policy on a piece of property. However as you have read from our case that is not always guaranteed. There are exceptions and we will point out how you can help improve your odds of receiving the benefits of the Title Insurance Policy.

A Title Commitment is equivalent to a binder for other types of insurance, which commits, or binds, the insurance company to issue the policy as set forth in the commitment.

The Title Commitment is organized into five main parts:

1. Who is being insured—generally, the lender and any future investors are the insureds, along with the purchasers of the property, assuming an Owner's Policy is being issued.

2. The amount of the insurance—usually the loan amount for the mortgagee and the sales price for the owner.

3. What is being insured—the legal description of the property

4. What is required to insure the title

   - Proof of taxes paid.

   - The Sellers'/Owners' Affidavit, to be signed at closing, indicating that the Seller/Owner is not aware of any facts or circumstances which would adversely affect title to the property.

   - Cancellation of any open mortgages, judgments or liens that the abstractor found bearing against the property.

   - Survey of the property by a licensed surveyor or a survey waiver to be signed at closing.

5. What is not insured—those matters affecting the property which in some way limit the free use of the property, usually called exceptions. Most exceptions are customary and do not affect the marketability of the property. Some of the typical exceptions in a policy include:

   - Servitudes/Easements—the right, usually granted to a utility company, to make limited use of a portion of the property to serve the insured property, as well as neighboring properties.

   - Restrictions/Covenants—rules and regulations, usually established by the developer of the subdivision, which prohibit property owners in the subdivision from doing things which could have a detrimental effect on quality of life or property values.

   - Oil, Gas and Mineral Titles—in Louisiana, mineral rights are governed by an exceptionally complex set of laws. In most cases, therefore, the title company will not insure for mineral rights.

   - Miscellaneous exceptions—the title insurance may not cover any unusual findings about a piece of property; these exceptions will be pointed out by the title agent/attorney.

It is important to understand that a commitment is typically not a comprehensive title search back to the original government land grant. In fact, the title insurance company will often make a business decision to insure certain risks without even disclosing them. As a result, a "clean" commitment does not necessarily indicate that the buyer will never have title problems--only that he will have coverage if problems do arise. For this reason, you should insist upon working with a reputable underwriter who will likely still be in business should a problem occur some years down the road.

The commitment is divided into four sections called "schedules," which are organized to provide information in a relatively standard format. (Other states use different formats.)

However, a quick once-over can give you some important information:

1. Are the buyers and/or sellers listed on the delivery slip? If not, they are not receiving copies of the commitment from the title company and it is incumbent upon the Realtor to deliver a copy.

2. Make sure all parties to the transaction are listed on the delivery slip. The lender and many attorneys that are involved will want to receive copies of the commitment.

3. Keep a copy of your delivery slip handy, because it lists your closer and your title contacts in case you have questions or issues prior to your c Closing.

Schedule A

"A" is for "Actual Facts." Schedule A contains basic information about the transaction. Here, you will find the effective date, the proposed policy coverage amount, the name of the current record title owner of the property, and a legal description of the property. There may be a problem if the amount, owner, or legal description varies from the contract terms. Likewise, if the effective date is well before closing, the buyer may wish to request an update to ensure that the information is current.

As soon as you receive your title commitment, carefully review the following information on Schedule A:

1. Are the buyers' names spelled correctly?

2. Is the purchase price correct?

3. Does the legal description match the one on the contract?

4. Are the sellers listed on the commitment the same parties who executed the contract?

5. Is the property address correct?

6. Does the title premium reflect a reissue rate if your seller is entitled to one?

7. If the contract calls for an Owner's Extended Coverage (OEC) policy, check the premium to make sure that the correct policy type is being paid for and provided.

8. Review the endorsements and make sure they apply to the property. Lender endorsements are requested by the lender and may not be removed by any other party.

If you find any discrepancies between Schedule A and the contract, let your closer know immediately.

Schedule B

Next comes Schedule B, "B" is for "Buyer Notification." which contains a preprinted list of standard exceptions that the title policy will not cover. Because much of this language is "boilerplate," some buyers tend to skim over Schedule B. This is a mistake. In addition to many preprinted terms, Schedule B will also list some matters specific to the transaction, including restrictive covenants, easements and rights-of-way, and mineral reservations. Any one of these items may seriously impair the usefulness of the property, so you should carefully review Schedule B and copies of any documents referenced there.

As soon as you receive your title commitment, carefully review the following information on Schedule B-1, Requirements:

1. Are any of the parties using a Power of Attorney? Even though there will not be a requirement listing this, it is very important to get a copy of the POA to your closer well in advance of the closing for review.

2. Is the seller or buyer a corporation, limited liability company, or partnership? If so, the requirements may call for a trade name affidavit, partnership agreement, or articles of incorporation. The sooner you can obtain these from your customer, the sooner the title department can review them.

Schedule C

"C" is for "Clear to Close. "Schedule C is often viewed as the "meat" of the commitment, and with good reason: it lists the requirements that must be satisfied for the issuance of the title policy. For example, the title company may require information regarding the marital status of one of the parties, copies of records from probates or bankruptcies, clarification of homestead status, or a new or updated survey. On Schedule C you will also find descriptions of mortgages, mechanic's liens, tax liens, judgments, lawsuits, assessments, and other such encumbrances affecting the title. The seller is primarily responsible for resolving exceptions noted in Schedule C.

Schedule D

"D" is for "Disclosure." Schedule D discloses basic information regarding ownership of the underwriter and the title company. Schedule D will also show the total policy premium, and a breakdown indicating how the premium is divided among the various parties who may be responsible for examining title and issuing the policy.

Request a "Marked-up" Title

This is a must as it can help in the event the Title Insurance Underwriter refuses to provide coverage in the event some exceptions are not satisfied. Does this sound familiar? Had we requested that the Title be "marked up" by their Agent it is plausible that the conditions and exceptions would be declared satisfied and the Title Insurance Policy issued thereby eliminating one of Ticors defense points.

In many areas of the country, it is customary for the title company or title agent to "mark-up" the commitment at closing to show which exceptions have been satisfied and/or waived and, therefore, will not appear on the final policy. Illinois and Texas are two examples. Many companies are trying to get to the point where their direct operations issue final policies at the closing as that streamlines their process, saves money and makes it less likely they will fall behind in issuing final policies during very busy times.

Of course, even in areas where the practice is common, a title insurance company could always take the position that the title agent was not authorized to do that for some reason. Logic may or may not enter into the insurer's position on that matter!

But consumers should be advised to ask for a "marked-up" commitment at closing. It takes a pretty savvy consumer, though to know whether that has been done and, if done, to know whether it has been done correctly in his or her case.

There aren't really any separate instructions apart from the normal requirements the agent or company has to see to remove an exception from a commitment. For example, if there's a mortgage or deed or trust the insurer will want a release, etc. There are two ways to "mark up" the commitment. First, the company or agent just writes "Waived" next to the item and initials it. Second, there is sometimes a "Waived" stamp which the company or agent stamps next to the item and the person using the stamp then initials the stamp.

There is also the situation where the exception remains in the policy but is insured over by way of endorsement. For example, a fence on the property might encroach onto the neighbor's land a couple of inches and the survey shows the encroachment so an exception is raised in the commitment.

The company will not remove the exception, but will, by way of endorsement, insure the buyer against loss suffered by reason of the entry of a court order denying the right to maintain the improvements in their current location.

The title commitment lays out the blueprint for the title policies. Marking it up indicates to the preparer of the policies that you have completed conditional items and how they should adjust the exceptions for the policies. For instance, Schedule B1 might say that you will subordinate a mortgage. By marking that item as "complied with" you are telling the file and anyone that needs to know, that you took care of it so they don't have to.

On Schedule B2, let's say you have an exception for restrictive covenants and the mortgage lender wants an endorsement covering any violations of covenants. You mark - or handwrite a note - on the Schedule B2 indicating which endorsement will be issued to cover that item in the loan policy.

Title Commitment - MUST HAVES

Understand the exceptions on the Title Commitment

Demand that the Title Agent/Attorney "mark-up" the Title Commitment stating that all exceptions have been satisfied

D. Title Insurance

We paid for Title Insurance as you saw on the HUD 1 shown in Chapter 3, yet Ticor is stating that we were only issued a Title Commitment and not a Title Insurance policy since all of the exceptions listed were not satisfied. We showed you in the previous chapter how to ensure that the exceptions become "satisfied" by demanding a marked-up title.

For us not to endorse Title Insurance will leave you even more exposed. The lesson here may be to not buy Title Insurance from an Underwriter who you know won't stand behind escrow theft problems that arise with their Agents. If you don't walk away from the closing table with the Title Insurance policy in hand they may very well walk away from you should a problem arise after you have closed.

Typically, a Title Insurance Policy will protect you against losses arising from problems connected to the title such as liens and defects. Make sure you have an owners policy that protects you for the full amount of the purchase. In order to receive a Closing Protection Letter you will need to purchase Title Insurance. Get the policy in-hand at the time you close. Do not walk away from the closing table without it. If you are located in a state where the deed must be recorded prior to issuance of the Title Policy then follow-up after the closing to obtain your policy as soon as possible. Even though the State of Michigan views the Title Commitment as a binder on the Title Insurance policy getting them to enforce this policy is another matter.

Before you purchased your home, it may have gone through several ownership changes, and the land on which it stands went through many more. There may be a weak link at any point in that chain that could emerge to cause trouble. For example, someone along the way may have forged a signature in transferring title. Or there may be unpaid real estate taxes or other liens. Title insurance covers the insured party for any claims and legal fees that arise out of such problems.

Title insurance is a form of insurance that is designed to protect lenders and property owners from any potential hidden claims against a property. If, for example, you purchase a home and later someone contends the sale was invalid, title insurance protects against any possible resulting losses.

Perhaps the owner, their family or their heirs have rights or claims in and to the property that you are buying. Others that may have an interest in or lien upon the property could include governmental bodies, contractors, lenders, judgment creditors, the Internal Revenue Service, or various other individuals or corporations. A property may be sold to you without the knowledge of the party having a right or claim in and to the property. These rights or claims remain attached to the title to the property that you are buying until they are rectified.

Title insurance is usually required by the lender to protect the lender against loss resulting from claims by others against your new home. In some states, attorneys offer title insurance as part of their services in examining title and providing a title opinion. The attorney's fee may include the title insurance premium. In other states, a title insurance company or title agent directly provides the title insurance.

Types of Title Insurance

There are two types of title insurance: Lenders title insurance, also known as a Loan Policy, and Owner's title insurance known as an owner's policy. Most lenders require a Loan Policy when they issue you a mortgage home loan when purchasing real estate. The Loan Policy is based on the dollar amount of your loan. It protects the lender's interests in the real estate should a problem with the title arise.

Owner's title insurance is normally issued in the amount of the real estate purchase. It is purchased for a one-time fee at closing and lasts as long as you or your heirs own the real estate. The Owner's title insurance fully protects the buyer should a problem arise with the title that was not uncovered during the title search. Owner's title insurance also pays for any legal fees involved in defending a claim to your title. Prices, and the way title insurance is issued, vary from state to state. Contact a title company in your state to see how it is handled.

Owner's Policy

The owner's policy insures buyers that the title to the real estate is free from all defects, liens and encumbrances except those which are listed as exceptions in the policy or are excluded from the policy's coverage. It also covers losses and damages suffered if the title is unmarketable. The policy also provides coverage for loss if there is no right of access to the land. These are the basic coverages and expanded residential owner's policy can be purchased that cover additional items of loss.

The liability limit of the owner's policy is typically the purchase price paid for the property. The policy may be paid by the seller or buyer as the parties agree; usually there is a custom in a particular state or county on this matter which is reflected in most local real estate contracts. Consumers should ask their Realtor the cost of title insurance before signing a real estate contract. Title insurance companies provide rate schedules to mortgage companies, real estate attorneys and lenders with detailed information as to the price of title insurance. Title insurance coverage lasts as long as the buyer retains an interest in the real estate insured.

Lender's Policy

Sometimes referred to as a loan policy and it is issued to mortgage lenders. It follows the assignment of the mortgage loan, meaning that the policy benefits the purchaser of the loan if the loan is sold. For this reason, these policies greatly facilitate the sale of mortgages into the secondary market. The secondary mortgage market is high volume purchasers like Fannie Mae and Federal Home Loan Mortgage Corporation including private institutions as well. Example of Insurance policy.

Title Insurance - MUST HAVES

Buy an Owners Title Insurance Policy

Request that you have the Title Insurance policy in hand at closing

E. Errors & Omissions Policy

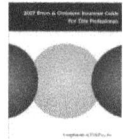

Another key piece of information that you should inquire with the Title Agent Title Attorney is proof that their Errors & Omissions (E&O) Policy is current. This will protect you against honest mistakes but will not cover purposefully mishandling of escrow money.

Our recommendation here is to demand a copy of the Title Agents/Attorneys E&O declaration page indicating that the policy is active. Look for the expiration date on the front page. If the Agent or Attorney takes offense to the request (which is on the Closing Checklist) then thank them for their time and find a different one. Do you really want to do business with them if they are not willing to show you proof of coverage.

Errors and Omissions (E&O) is the insurance that covers the Title Agent/Attorney in the event that a client holds them responsible for a service you provided, or failed to provide, that did not have the expected or promised results. For doctors, dentists, chiropractors, etc., it is often called malpractice insurance. For lawyers, accountants, architects or engineers, it may be called professional liability. Whatever you call it, it provides coverage for errors (or omissions) that were made or that the client perceives you have made.

Most E&O policies cover judgments, settlements and defense costs on behalf of the Title Agent. Even if the allegations are found to be groundless, thousands of dollars may be needed to defend the lawsuit. They can bankrupt a smaller company or individual and have a lasting effect on the bottom line of larger companies.

Some E&O policies provide a coverage feature called Fidelity or Criminal coverage. This coverage addresses the most common fidelity threats, including losses due to employee dishonesty, credit card forgery, computer fraud and theft, disappearance and destruction of property. Ask your Title Agent/Attorney if they have this coverage. This coverage may help improve your odds of recovery.

In short, E&O coverage provides protection for Title Agents/Attorneys in the event that an honest error or omission has caused a financial loss. Escrow theft is not typically a covered item however it will provide protection in the event of an honest mistake. Make sure they have it and it is current.

PolicyExample

P.01/01

ZURICH

Certificate of Insurance

Policy Number: EOC 5876620-00
Certificate Number: T1023600

Title Agents, Abstractors and Escrow Agents Errors and Omissions Liability Insurance Policy

This is a Claims Made and Reported Policy. Please review the Policy carefully. The policy is limited to liability for only those Claims that are first made against the Insured and reported to the Company during the Policy Period.

Item 1. Insured by the stock company below and hereinafter referred to as the **Company.**
Steadfast Insurance Company

Item 2.
CONSOLIDATED TITLE SERVICES LLC
20300 CIVIC CENTER DR #302
SOUTHFIELD MI 48076

Item 3. Policy Period From: 4/29/2003 To: 4/29/2004 12:01 A.M. Standard Time at the address of the Named Insured as stated herein.	**Item 4.** Limit of Liability Each Claim: $ 500,000 Aggregate: $ 1,000,000
	Item 5. Deductible $ $10,000.00
Item 6. Premium: $9,596.00	**Item 7.** Premium Tax $239.90

Item 8. Retroactive Date   4/29/1997

Item 9. Forms Attached at Issue:

This Certificate of Insurance is issued off the Master Policy held by the Members of the Title Agents of America Purchasing Group. By acceptance of this policy, the Certificate Holder agrees that the statements in the certificate and the application and any attachments hereto are the Certificate Holder's agreements and representations and that this policy embodies all agreements existing between the Certificate Holder and the Company or any of its representatives relating to this insurance.

Notice to Company
Zurich North America – Specialties Claims
Attn.: Professional Liability Claim Department
P.O. Box 307010
Jamaica, NY 11430-7010

Issue Date: 6/6/2003 Authorized Representative:	Date:

INSURED COPY

2003-05

TOTAL P.01

60

Errors & Omissions Insurance - MUST HAVES

Demand a copy of the Title Agent/Attorney E&O declaration page to verify their policy is in force

If they refuse or don't have E&O find another Title Agent/Attorney

F. Closing Protection Coverage

If you remember nothing else from this book remember these three letters CPL. These stand for **C**losing **P**rotection **L**etter. Every time you purchase or sell a property you must <u>demand a Closing Protection Letter</u>. When you purchase Title Insurance and have a CPL in hand the Title Insurance Underwriter is backing the actions of the Title Agent /Attorney. If the money is mishandled on purpose or liens are not paid off the Title Insurance Underwriter should stand behind your claim.

You should request that the CPL come directly from the Title Insurance Underwriter not the Title Agent or Attorney. This will help prevent the Title Insurance Underwriter from claiming that the Agent or Attorney lacked the authority to issue such a letter.

When you request a CPL some Title Agents or Closing Attorneys may say they provide them to Lenders but not consumers. <u>This simply is just not true.</u> Have them make a phone call to their Underwriter if necessary. A CPL is a MUST HAVE if you are buying or selling.

A CPL, sometimes referred to as an insured closing letter, is a document issued by title insurance underwriters that sets forth an underwriter's responsibility for negligence, fraud and errors in closings performed by agents and approved attorneys.

Without this piece of paper everything could be at risk. Your money, the home you are buying or selling, everything. Banks and lenders are well aware of the risk when money is wired into the account of Title Agents/Attorneys for the home purchase. <u>Lenders are smart.</u> First, they demand that Consumer buys a Lenders Title Insurance policy and second, they demand that Title Underwriter provide them with Closing Protection on the funds they are wiring into the Title Agents/Attorneys escrow accounts.

This IS the secret Title Underwriters don't want you to know about. The reason is simple. They don't want to assume the risk for their Title Agent network yet they have been forced to do so by the Lenders and Banks. If you demand a CPL and they refuse then refuse to close, delay the closing while you find a Title Agent who will provide what you are asking for. <u>It is really that important.</u> If we had a CPL in our case the Title Underwriter may have settled with us long ago.

Following is an example for what a CPL looks like. They will issue it to you if you demand one. If not find another Title Agent.

Closing Protection Letter Example

OLD REPUBLIC
National Title Insurance Company

Independence Office:
6480 Rockside Woods Blvd. South
Independence, Ohio 44131
Voice: 216-524-5700 -- Fax Number: 216-5242700
Toll Free: 800-321-0520
Email: ICL.RR@OldRepNatl.com

Liberty Savings Bank, F.S.B.,
its successors and/or assigns, as their interest may appear

Pertaining To:

Binder/Order Number:
Covered Parties:

Seller Name:	☐	
Buyer Name:	☐	
Lender Name:	☑	LIBERTY SAVINGS BANK, F.S.B.
Borrower Name:	☑	

Closing Protection Coverage on Behalf of:

OHIO TITLE CORPORATION COLUMBUS
AGENCY, INC.
155 W. MAIN STREET, SUITE 200
COLUMBUS OH 43215
614-221-7701 - PHONE
HEATHER ROBINSON - AGENT CONTACT
bnorris@ohiotitlecolumbus.com

Re: Ohio Closing Protection Coverage

Dear Customer:

When title insurance is specified in connection with closings of the above-described real estate transaction (the "Closing") in which you are the Covered Party with an interest in land or a lender secured by a mortgage (including any other security instrument) of an interest in land, Old Republic National Title Insurance Company (the "Company"), subject to the Conditions and Exclusions set forth below, hereby agrees to reimburse you for actual loss incurred by you in connection with the Closing, when such Closing is conducted by the above named Licensed Agent (an agent licensed and authorized to issue title insurance in the State of Ohio for the Company) and where such loss arises out of:

1. Theft, misappropriation, fraud or any other failure of the Licensed Agent, or anyone acting on the Licensed Agent's behalf, to properly disburse or otherwise, in the handling of your funds or documents in connection with such Closing to the extent such fraud or dishonesty relates to the status of the title to said interest in land or the marketability thereof as insured, or to the validity, enforceability, and priority of the lien of said mortgage on said interest in land; or

2. Failure of the Licensed Agent, or anyone acting on the Licensed Agent's behalf, to comply with any applicable written closing instructions, when agreed to by the Licensed Agent, to the extent that they relate to: (a) the status of the title to said interest in land or the marketability thereof as insured or the validity, enforceability and priority of the lien on said mortgage said interest in land, including the obtaining of documents and the disbursement of funds necessary to establish such status of title or the lien; or (b) the obtaining of any other document, specifically required by you, but only to the extent the failure to obtain such other document affects the status of the title to said interest in land or the validity, enforceability and priority of the lien of said mortgage on said interest in land, but not to the extent that said instructions require a determination of the validity, enforceability or effectiveness of such other

document.

CONDITIONS AND EXCLUSIONS

A. The Company will not be liable to you for loss arising out of:

    1. Loss or impairment of your funds in the course of collection or while on deposit with a bank due to bank failure, insolvency or suspension, except such as shall result from failure of the Licensed Agent to comply with your written closing instructions to deposit the funds in a bank which you designated by name.

    2. Mechanics' and materialmen's liens in connection with your purchase or lease or construction loan transactions, except to the extent that protection against such liens is afforded by a title insurance binder, commitment or policy.

    3. Matters created, suffered, assumed or agreed to by you and/or your agents or employees.

B. Should the Company reimburse you pursuant to this CPC, it shall be subrogated to all rights and remedies which you would have had against any person or property had you not been so reimbursed. Liability of the Company for such reimbursement shall be reduced to the extent that your have knowingly and voluntarily impaired the value of such right of subrogation.

C. Any liability of the Company for loss incurred by you in connection with the Closing by a Licensed Agent shall be limited to the protection provided by this CPC. However, this CPC shall not affect nor be deemed to be a substitute for the protection afforded by a title insurance binder, commitment or policy.

D. Liability under this CPC to a covered buyer, borrower, or lender is limited to the amount of applicable owner's or lender's policy of title insurance, and any payment under this CPC shall constitute a payment under the applicable policy of title insurance to the extent such payment is for a matter also covered under said policy.

E. Liability under this CPC to a covered seller is limited to actual loss of funds and shall in no event be greater than the gross sales price due the seller in the covered transaction.

F. Claims shall be made promptly to the Company at its principal office at 400 Second Avenue South, Minneapolis, Minnesota 55401-2499. When the failure to give prompt notice shall prejudice the Company, then liability of the Company hereunder shall be reduced to the extent of such prejudice.

G. The Company shall not be liable hereunder unless notice of claim in writing is received by the Company within one year from the date of the Closing.

H. The scope and effect of this CPC is limited to a single transaction, which is the Closing on the commitment or binder referenced in the caption.

I. This CPC supercedes any previously issued closing protection letter(s) or CPC.

OLD REPUBLIC NATIONAL TITLE INSURANCE COMPANY
By:

Robert Wasserman
Vice President

cf: HEATHER ROBINSON

Closing Protection Letter - MUST HAVES

Demand that a CPL be provided to you either prior to or at closing

Demand that the CPL come directly from the Title Underwriter

This is probably the most important Must Have in this entire book !

G. Post Closing Follow-Up

Don't overlook this critical step. If the seller's bank does not receive the full payoff on the existing mortgage they will not release the mortgage. This means you won't own the home and the seller may not have sold their home causing problems for both sides. It's a shame that you need to do this but had we followed up to make sure the lien holders received payment and they were satisfied we could have discovered the problem early on and reduced our exposure.

If proceeds are wired to the lender ask for a confirmation statement that the money wire was both sent and received. Do not leave the closing table with out. If a certified check is sent overnight to the lender ask the Title Agent to obtain a letter from the lender (on the lenders letterhead) that the money has been received AND the previous mortgage satisfied. This is included on the "Closing Checklist", just remind the Title Agent at the closing table of this requirement.

Mark your calendar two weeks after closing to call the county "Register of Deeds" office in which you closed to verify that the Deed has been recorded. If they can't provide you with the information then start calling the Title Agent to find out why.

Post Closing Follow-up - MUST HAVES

Demand proof that the funds were wired and received by the sellers bank

Request that your Title Agent/Attorney provide you with confirmation that the previous mortgage has been discharged

Follow-up after the closing to with register of deeds office to ensure that the deed has been received and is being recorded

H. Legal Help

A good source is to check with your states local bar association for Real Estate Attorneys in your area. Another good source is your Realtor (if you have one) for finding an experienced Attorney whom they have used successfully in the past. As a last resort, Google search for Real Estate Attorney's in your area. We suggest you have your closing docs reviewed by this Attorney prior to closing.

With Attorney fees ranging from $195 – $300+ per hour it won't take long to mount huge legal expense fighting to get your money back. We have over $50,000.00 racked up in legal fees so far.

One alternative to reducing your exposure is to purchase Pre-Paid Legal (PPL). This is a national company, traded on the stock exchange that provides good value for the money.

If you are buying, selling, or renting homes PPL can provide access to an Attorney for many issues not just real estate. Use the internet to search for Pre- Paid Legal to review the available plans and benefits.

Legal Help - MUST HAVES

Have a qualified Real Estate Attorney review your docs in advance of closing

Consider Pre-Paid Legal plan coverage to reduce your exposure

---

CHAPTER 10

Final Thoughts

There is no doubt if you do the steps outlined in Chapter 9 "How To Prevent This From Happening To You" and utilize the Closing Checklist you will significantly reduce your risk and improve your ability to recover quickly should you be a victim of escrow theft.

Currently as of this writing our case is in the hands of the Court of Appeals. If they rule in our favor then our case goes back to the trial court for an actual trial. If they rule in Ticor's favor we will continue our fight to drive legislative change on a national level. This is really what needs to happen in order to protect home buyers and sellers nationally.

Before we close, just stop and think for a minute about the real estate closing network in the United States. Like most insurance regulation there is nothing united about it. Each state has it's own way of doing things which creates significant risk for consumers. Lenders and Title Underwriters know this very well. In all but a couple of states there are networks of Title Agents/Attorneys who handle billions of dollars annually yet they have very little regulation.

This lack of regulation, oversight and training among Title Agents has created integrity issues with some. This causes innocent home buyers and sellers to pay the price for their dishonesty and misappropriation of money that does not belong to them.

Title Underwriters stand watching from the sidelines as consumers get ripped off by the Agency networks they established to fill their coffers with insurance premiums.

Our goal is to drive change on a national level that will force the Title Underwriters to ensure their Agents are properly trained, audited and regulated so <u>consumers have zero risk.</u> If they want to continue using this Issuing Agent network they should be the ones responsible for making it a safe place to do business.

We believe that God has placed us in this situation for a reason. That reason, we believe, is to use our knowledge and contacts within the industry, corporate experience and passion to drive change on this issue.

The future plans call for raising national awareness on this issue and building accountability and integrity in the current process to ensure consumers are fully protected.

We are on a mission to fix this problem. Short term we want all of our money back so we can pay the people we owe and get our lives back. Longer term we want to build awareness for this issue and drive change within the industry.

Now that <u>you know the secret</u> of how banks and lenders receive protection for their money from Title Underwriters you to can receive the same protection. Follow the steps we have outlined so you don't experience years of financial hardship from losing your home and your money at closing.

If you have had a similar experience or have comments about this subject we would like to hear from you. Go to **www.SafeHomePurchase.com** click on "Contact us" and send us an email. If we can help, we certainly will. Together we will make a difference.

God Bless

Paul & LaDonna Szatkowski

www.ingramcontent.com/pod-product-compliance
Lightning Source LLC
Chambersburg PA
CBHW021915190326
41519CB00008B/790